ADVANC

Cassie shares game-changing truths in her latest book. This law of attraction money maven will inspire you to not just be excited about your big dreams again, but show you the clear way there. In my experience, time spent with Cassie is well invested and easy to appreciate. Let her rock your world in all the best ways!

JEANNETTE MAW
Good Vibe Coach, GoodVibeUniversity.com

In all my years of studying LOA + the people who teach it, I have NEVER seen anyone who designs their life the way Cassie does.

I've known her from her earliest days and been witness to her meteoric rise to become one of the top Money Manifesting coaches around.

And here's her 'secret'... laid out in clear + precise detail.

Truthfully, it's not really a secret. Lots of coaches talk about scripting + its immense magic. But Cassie has dissected it into a formula, a recipe for life alchemy, in a way that is both insanely useful + epically inspiring.

You know that fairy-tale ending you've yearned for?

Cassie Parks can help you not only write it... but LIVE it.

JACQUELINE GATES
LOA Nesting

As a long-time student of the Law of Attraction, I've read many, many books on the subject. I'm thrilled that Cassie Parks' latest book "Lifestyle Design for a Champagne Life" has a place way up there in my top ten. In this concise, no-nonsense, easy-to-read volume, Cassie sets out exactly what makes LOA work in the real world, and then teaches the approach she used herself, to create her dream life. There's just enough technical information of LOA and brain science to satisfy the sceptical left brain, a clear step by step explanation of her process (which, by the way, is brilliant!), and plenty of juicy examples to draw the reader in. I read the book in a single sitting because I couldn't put it down, but I've already scheduled three days to try her process out for myself. Why three days? If you want to know that, you'll have to read the book! Highly recommended for anyone who wants to know how to apply LOA in a powerful, clear and focused way.

JANETTE DALGLIESH
Identity Shift Ninja

Cassie Parks expands the understanding of the Law of Attraction (LOA) to work for you. She has developed a new technique based her own experiences. The method "Scripting Your Champagne Days" is so detailed that everything you need to know is in this book. It's full of examples of how to do it and how not to, the latter useful.

The method goes way beyond story telling, it takes you further than that. So far that you will become a master of LOA.

It's the missing link to "The Secret", yes, it's that good.

Cassie is not afraid of telling her own story with years of failure getting the Law of Attraction to work for her. I could relate while reading it. The difference is that she found the missing link.

This is a book I will recommend to everyone I know, even those who are already good at attracting what they want of life.

SUSANNE FLOW

"Loved this book!! As someone who has manifested many things over the years, I never figured out what I was doing to have things fall into place. This book clearly spells out the exact steps. Loved the formula, the on-the-spot reporting concept, and bringing it together from so many different angles. Loved the detail of the scripting!! The biggest "aHa" for me was not to script the how, but rather the feeling state. Yes the Universe will put together a much better plan than I could ever imagine. I'm excited to see what magic shows up for me next and I'm sure it will happen a lot faster!"

WENDY WERNER

"Cassie has a wonderful knack for taking a technique and bringing it completely to life. If you've heard of scripting and think it probably is valuable...but haven't quite managed to use it effectively, check out this book! I have been scripting for years, with mixed results, but Scripting Your Champagne Life Story takes it to a depth I'd never experienced before. I got 'aha' after 'aha' reading this book - I can see that in the past I have done too little, too late; and changing that pattern is already yielding results. I'm already looking forward to the next one in the series"

DONNA, UK
http://www.donnaonthebeach.com

Finally, encouragement, technique, and clear instructions for the Law of Attraction.

"Lifestyle Design for a Champagne Life" is a glorious garden where I've found clear understanding and Cassie Parks is a rose among the thorns! I was about to give up on my manifesting efforts and sadly let life continue to repeat itself one familiar day at a time. I have bought printed books, e-books, followed blogs, enrolled in courses, and watched countless YouTube videos. Through my constant collecting of information, believing I had not yet found the right resource, and inability to stay focused, I decided all I need to do is be grateful, meditate, feel good, raise my vibration, speak affirmations, act as if, avoid negativity, journal, keep my vision board current, make mind movies, script, don't worry about the how but don't think don't because that brings more don't instead of do, clear my past, spend 5 minutes doing this, 15 minutes doing that, and do the hokey pokey and turn myself around.

Finally, encouragement, technique, and clear instructions melded together in fifty (50) fantastic pages! Thank you, Cassie Parks!! You're a life-changer!!

ELAINE RAGSDALE LEE

"Brilliant! I'm so grateful for this book. Just love it. I had so many Ah-Ha moments. Things that I've heard before and understood intellectually just sunk in and I really got "it" (it being the LOA and my power and part in it). There is also plenty of new imperative information that I never heard before as well. The authors easy way with words and stories spoke to me clearly and powerfully. This book has left me feeling excited, assured and confident in my powers to attract. This is a brilliant, smart, and inspired book and I will read it again for sure. I'm so glad to have found it!"

ML

The Book, Lifestyle Design for a Champagne Life is a great demonstration of how to work the Law of Attraction into your life. I loved the reminder that we are all here to live the life of our dreams and Cassie created an easy to understand and fun to do, step-by- step on how to live a life that is completely satisfying and a vibrational match for what is in your heart. I must say what an inspiration the book has been and has dropped into my life at just the right time! Being reminded that there is a choice in the life that you desire and all that is needed is the time to design it. Design, Declare it, and watch it all unfold.

JULIE JARNOT NGUYEN

This book is genius! The author skillfully guides the reader through a very detailed process of attraction. It has been a long time since I have felt so beautifully sucked into a book as I did with this one. Cassie Parks has a remarkable talent of drawing clients and readers deeply into the very soul of the creation process. Highly recommended, this book was a very inspirational read for me.

STACY GOWER

'Ever wanted to create your dream life but not really know how? If you've been frustrated by not getting the results you want in utilizing the Law of Attraction, then this book will part the clouds, so you can step into your vision easily.

Cassie Parks has done a wonderful job of guiding the reader step by step to create the life of their dreams. With such an open and honest appraisal of her own life journey, Cassie shows you how easy it can be to live your dream life now. Inspirational! Couldn't put it down!'

FLEUR MILLER

"This is a positive, friendly manual for creating an excellent life that is easy to relate to. Cassie shows how concentrating on the end result, what you really want out of all your thoughts about what to manifest, can help you ease up on trying to control the path the manifestation takes, which opens up space for the universe to do its thing and create the perfect path toward your goal. Her step-by-step process helps you zero in on what you really want, setting you well on your way toward that dream."

JESSICA SPRINGER

Law of Attraction, a power vested in all but very few know how to make it use. This book "Life Style Design of Champagne Life" by Cassie Parks gives a clear guideline to achieve the much sought after abundance in our life. She has in very simple words given us the key to gaining abundance or in her words living the Champagne Life. Abundance in the form of love, riches, health or any desire which can be attracted by all of us.

I loved the way she shared her life story and how she ended getting what she desired. She mentioned that many of us already attract what we desire in one sector but in the other sector no matter how hard we try lady luck never shines. For example a person may attract love or good health without even noticing that he or she is attracting it but may never be able to attract finance or good friends. This statement stands very true for me, I have always been the person who could attract the person I would have a crush on and get into a relationship with him. I could think of that person and next thing you know he has asked me out on a date. This may take sometimes a month or few months, a year or few years and in some cases even an hour would be enough. I had a crush on my now husband since school days but I never told him about it. After school lost all my contacts but he always on my mind. 11 years later got back touch with him thanks to technology and now we are married for last 3 years.

However, when it came to wealth, I am always trying to settle financially, which after reading this book is making me realise that I may need to look at the innermost desire which was my dream of working by choice and not due to any obligation, spending time with friends and family, travelling and this book has shown me the pathway to reach my intended destination. I have read many Law of Attraction books but none felt this close to heart. It was as if the writer was talking to me and guiding me for the changes I need to make. I am a great believer that reading this book was a sign by the universe to help me attract what I desire. Thank you Cassie for sharing your experience and wisdom with all us. Highly recommend this book to anyone who would love living a Champagne Life but hasn't been able to attract it yet.

CHARLOTTE D.

I have enjoyed all Cassie's books but this one, I have enjoyed even more. In this book, she shares with us her genuine story, not from the point of view of the Guru of someone who knows for sure all about the Law of Attraction, but from her own and real personal story, sharing with us her fears and mistakes. I really appreciate this because it helps me understand why sometimes things do not work as we would like them to. With this book, Cassie helps you to refocus and get back on track so that you can attract all you desire and what you have defined as your ChampagneLife. It is an easy book to read, simple but profound and with a lot of tips and exercises to get you in action.

ERIKA WASSINK

This book resonated with me on so many levels! Cassie offers several practical exercises to help you design your own "Champagne Life". The book is very easy to understand and it's one of the most inspirational books on LOA that I've read. LOVE this book!

TRACY MORROW HATHCOCK
Author

I just read Cassie Parks new book Lifestyle Design For a Champagne Life and loved it! Very easy to understand, I really recommend everyone looking to change their mindset, this is the book to read!

GLORIA DELFIN

I loved this book. This is the first time that creating life on my terms has been revealed in such an easy to understand way. The exercises are laid out in an effortless way to implement everything that is learned. I was able to really connect with myself in a deeper level with the feelings I want for my champagne life. Thank you.

I really loved the book and want to reread it to connect on a deeper level.

TRICIA DYCKA

Lifestyle Design

for a
Champagne Life

---

*Find Out Why the Law of Attraction
Isn't Working, Learn the Secret to
Lifestyle Design, and Make Your
Dream a Reality*

BY CASSIE PARKS

difference press

TABLE OF CONTENTS

INTRODUCTION TO
YOUR CHAMPAGNE LIFE

You are smart and beautiful. You're passionate. You are a good friend. You know about the Law of Attraction. You might have seen *The Secret* or watched *What the Bleep*. You may have heard of Abraham or Jeannette Maw (she's one of my favorites). You get the idea. Like attracts like. You know the Law of Attraction (LOA) isn't something that works or doesn't; it's working all the time, whether or not you are aware of it, whether or not you intentionally activate it. I understand what it feels like to work all the LOA tools, be dedicated, try your best, and not get the results you are craving.

You believe you can manifest things–and you have. You have done it once or twice. Maybe a whole lot of times. Parking places might be your specialty, or maybe it's a knack for getting to the front of the line wherever you go. You might even be a master at manifesting what you desire for free.

You totally get that it works, because you've seen proof in your life and in others' lives. Maybe you love manifesting free stuff already, but it's just not that exciting anymore because you're ready to grow. You want more. You desire more. Even if you have had some success with manifesting bigger things, you'd like more. Or maybe you can't seem to manifest the bigger, better stuff you desire. Maybe it isn't even "stuff" at all that you desire now. You desire an experience, a relationship, your dream job, a life that fulfills you.

While you get the process and you pretty much get how to manifest the "stuff," it's the other stuff—the stuff of your deepest desires—that's the stuff you're not quite sure how to manifest. Or what you're trying just isn't working. So now what? Should you focus on this or that? How do you know if you're doing it right? How do you know when to stay the course and when to change what you're doing? There are *so* many techniques and so many versions of what you "should" do, how do you know which one to follow? How do you know what, exactly, to do to get you into your dream life with less trial and error?

I understand that desire... and that frustration. I call your "dream life" your Champagne Life. Your Champagne Life is the one that is worth sipping and savoring. It's a life that, at the end of each day, makes you feel like you had the best day ever, even if nothing extraordinary happened. It's a life you deem worth celebrating... every day. It's that life you have been dreaming of living.

The thing about your dream life is that if you can dream it, it's possible. In fact, I believe it already exists, it's just waiting for you to come true. I know you have been looking for that "missing piece" of the manifesting puzzle to make it come true. You keep trying everything you can think of, because you, too, know your Champagne Life is out there. You just have to draw it into you. You *can* draw it into you, using the magic of the Law of Attraction.

Albert Einstein said, "Everything is a miracle, or nothing is a miracle." There is science to back up the Law of Attraction. I believe it is science, but I also believe everything is a miracle. Believing in miracles makes me believe the Law of Attraction is magic. I prefer to believe in magic. I think magic makes life more fun. Whether you see the Law of Attraction as purely scientific or as pure magic, you can leverage its power to draw your dream life into your existence now.

Clients who come to me for an LOA Tune-Up often know way more than I do. They know techniques I've never even heard of. They do way more than I do, and yet they come to me because they are not getting what they want. They are not able to put the pieces together to get the outcomes they want.

There is often one of three things going on. One, some of these people are working too hard. They are doing all the things they've been taught will get results, but not really getting any benefit from them, so they become frustrated... and exhausted. Two, they know so much but they don't quite get around to putting anything into practice. This is usually because they find a new technique, do it for awhile, and do not get the results they want quickly, so they move onto a new technique. After a few cycles of this they just stop trying, because they do not know how to make it work to receive what they desire. Third, some people do not have a clear vision of what they want after all. They are trying to manifest bits and pieces of things they think they desire, but, without the whole picture, manifesting can be tricky or even attract the "wrong" things.

You are beautiful, amazing, and fully capable of utilizing the Law of Attraction to create your Champagne Life. I know that because you are reading this book. I know that because I am going to teach you how to put your magic to its best use.

EXERCISE

Before we go any further, let's talk about what that beautiful, amazing thing you desire is. Whether it's a new car or an entire life, take a few minutes to close your eyes and visualize it.

- What do you see?

- How clear is the picture?

- How connected do you feel to your desire?

- How possible does it feel?

When you open your eyes, rate the last three questions on a scale of 1–10 for how clear, connected and possible they feel. Being in the range of 8–10 will vastly improve your chances of attracting your desire. Keep reading, because we're going to get you closer to a 10.

LISTEN TO
Manifest it Now
ON ITUNES

LEARN MORE
ABOUT
PUTTING
THESE
PRINCIPLES
INTO ACTION

IT HASN'T ALWAYS BEEN MAGIC FOR ME

I understand what it feels like to be doing all the things you can think of, yet not getting what you want. Several years ago, I started helping people shift their thoughts and beliefs to attract *less* of what they didn't want and *more* of what they did. While I loved the work, my practice was small. It was mostly my group of friends and a few people my sister referred to me. In fact, it arguably wasn't much of a practice and was a little more like a hobby.

One day, my friend, who was also a housemate, came to me and said, "I want to do 10 sessions to get over my ex." Being the amazing creator that I am, I suggested everyone living in the house could use some clearing out of the old and inviting in of new relationships, and that I would create a weekend-long Attracting Love Workshop for us all to try as a group.

My housemates agreed and I started creating it. We had graduation parties and other things to attend the upcoming weekend, but we all agreed we would devote the time to the workshop as well. This workshop was awesome. We set intentions. We shared video clips so we would have visual representations of what we wanted. We released fears about love. We identified all the features we wanted in our respective new relationships. We made the most amazing vision boards, using the chakras as guides, for identifying how we wanted to think, act, and feel about our future partners.

It was an amazing weekend. Everyone felt open and refreshed during and afterward, and we were all excited to see what would happen. Within two months, my friend had attracted her soulmate. They were married within two years. When I asked my friend if her wife was everything we had put out there during the workshop, she said, "Yes, and more." Yay for her. I was sure my guy was coming.

Six months later, nothing. Not even a glimmer of him. I started to wonder what I was doing wrong. I had the vision board hanging in my room. I looked at it every day. I had set the intentions. I had made the list of what I wanted. I had cleared my fears. I had even energetically shifted to be "on" for attracting all the things I wanted. I couldn't figure out what I was doing wrong.

I was so determined there must be some other belief I needed to fix, that I went to more than one of someone else's love workshops. I did all the work. I shared my fears. I set my intentions... over and over again.

I convinced myself it was just going to take more time. About a year after the workshop, I sat down and looked at the vision board anew. I was bound and determined to figure out what I was doing wrong that was keeping him from showing up in my life.

That's when I saw it. The first thing I had written on my vision board at the top was, "Supports my work." That was it. That is what I was doing wrong. I wasn't doing my work. How could I attract a guy who supported my work, if I had one client every two months, which meant basically I was not *doing* my work. By *my work*, I meant what I came here to do. Not the job I was working at the time.

If I wanted a soulmate who supported "my work," I knew I would have to start doing my work more consistently. I went to work building my business. I put it out there, I wanted my business to be my full-time thing. I set the intentions. I cleared the fears and limiting beliefs, and I went to work on every level, making the necessary investment and trying to build my business to sustain the life my guy would eventually be part of.

I visualized. I wrote down what I wanted. I constantly worked on myself to release all the negative beliefs I had. I traded coaching sessions with someone else who does similar work. I started focusing on my money mindset, because I wanted to engage paying clients so that I could make enough money to support myself and leave my job, and of course so that I could then manifest my soulmate.

I was committed. I was *acting as if* (or so I thought). I paid $7500 to attend a week-long business training, because that is what I was told big business people do. I wrote a book, because I wanted to speak and do workshops, and I was told I needed a book if I was going to be a speaker. All of this seemed like I was *acting as if*, because all the speakers I knew about had books.

I hired a marketing person, because I was acting like a business owner and I have a degree in psychology and not marketing. I flew to places and coached at workshops for free because I thought I was *acting as if*. I enrolled in a training that was supposed to teach me how to be a speaker and make money at it. It cost $5000.

Throughout this time, alongside all the spending and *acting as if*, I was doing visualizations. I was setting my intentions. I had a gratitude journal. I continued fixing my negative thoughts and beliefs. I had a different friend at this point who I exchanged sessions with. I was doing a lot of sessions with her, and on myself for that matter, to "fix" whatever was keeping me from manifesting enough clients to leave my job.

On top of the internal work I was doing, I was working really hard. I wasn't always sure what I was doing, but I was working long hours at night and skipping fun things on the weekend because I believed business owners work hard. I was ok with working hard, because I believed that was what I had to do to get my business running. I know now that that doesn't have to be true. Work doesn't always require all of our time, or have to be hard.

Once my book was out and I was gaining a little bit of momentum, the momentum got shut down. It became clear that there was not going to be any flexibility whatsoever at my job for things that had to do with building my business. I wondered what I had done wrong, and how I had manifested that roadblock, when I'd been working so hard.

I kept going. I kept trying to fix my thoughts and beliefs, and I kept hiring people to help me with my business. I had a good business set up, LovingYourselfUniversity.com. I had great contributors and a good idea. I was passionate about that idea. It felt inspired. And I was going to create a passive income with it. It was awesome. I did a lot of work. I did a lot of marketing. And yet, I think I made a grand total of $47 profit off that site. That is even after all the intentions I set. At first, I was too frustrated to see what I was doing wrong.

It turned out that I simply wasn't looking in the right places for evidence of success, because all I saw was my frustration. About six months ago, I found a handful of comments on LovingYourselfUniversity.com that I had completely missed. Some from people who wanted to pay me. Some from people who wanted me to speak at events. I literally had not seen them when I was engaged in working that business, because I was so focused on "trying" to make it work and on the fact that it "wasn't working." It *was* working, but I just couldn't see it because I was constantly *trying* to make it work. I could not even see that it was working. I wanted to be paid and one of the comments was someone wanting to pay me. I missed it, because my sole focus was on it not working.

A passive income was the way I thought I was going to get out of my job. If I could create enough passive income products, I could get out. You always get better results running toward something rather than away from something, but

I didn't know that yet. I kept trying to figure out how to do it through more hard work and expecting something to hit big.

Then, one day, after trapping myself inside all weekend working instead of having fun, I threw my hands up. Building a coaching practice was not working. I believed I was using LOA. I was working really hard and it just wasn't giving me the results I intended. I decided it wasn't going to work, ever. I gave up on my dream that day, because I didn't want it if it was going to keep me from enjoying the rest of my life.

On one hand, that was a really sad day. On the other hand, it was probably the first time I had let go in 5 years. Letting go felt like a weight had been lifted off my shoulders. I took a deep breath and actually felt oxygen expand my lungs for the first time in a very, very long time. All this hard work had created a stifling, anxious, stressful state of being, and that itself certainly contributed to attracting resistance to my own intentions. If that was what getting my dream life was going to feel like, it was actually feeling kind of crappy.

Letting go opened space, allowing me to step back and ask the single most important question you can ask yourself, "What do I really want?" For years, I had been trying to "make" something (my business) happen because I thought it would "make" something else (my soul mate showing up) happen. It had been over 5 years since I asked myself what my dream life really looked like.

What did I really want? To be financially independent. I wanted to make enough passive income that I got to choose if I woke up and went to work or not. I had wanted that since I was 19 years old, when I realized that was a thing people did. That was almost 10 years prior. My dream wasn't about millions and millions of dollars, big fancy cars and houses. It was about choice and freedom.

It's important to remember that I had been working on my money mindset all along. Only I wasn't forcing my money mindset like I was forcing my business into existence. I wasn't focused on how it *wasn't* working. It was fun to play with. It was actually easy to play with, because I didn't have a need to make it work. I was very focused on shifting my thoughts about money, but that became more like a game instead of something I was forcing myself to do to get something else.

My money mindset had actually shifted quite nicely and I had manifested raises. They came with more work and more stress, but I was happy to have expanded my money beliefs to be able to receive what I thought was a lot of money at that point. I was making really good choices with my money and had all my debt paid off and was growing a big savings account.

Once I realized what I really wanted was to be financially free, it was easy to open to that possibility. That feeling of freedom was so easy to tap into. It was easy to *act as if* I had all the money I needed to be able to choose whether I wanted to go to work or not. I had downsized a few years earlier and purchased a smaller house to live in as part of something I learned at a money mindset course. I kept the house I had been living in and rented it out, so I had some small investment income and a property that someone else (the renter) was paying the mortgage on. Then a few years later, following my feel-good, I moved downtown and rented out the second house I had purchased, so I had some more investment income. Knowing I wanted to pay those houses off faster, I would put extra money towards the payments. I had this game I would play, where I would run numbers really far out (10-20 years) and then the houses would be paid off and I would have all this money that I got to choose what to do with. It felt *so* good to play in that space. I did it all time. That vibration was *so* easy to step into.

In less than a year, I was financially independent, because I actually used my LOA magic on that. I told people the story of being financially independent. I talked about leaving my job. I felt that feeling of freedom *all* the time. I tapped that magic pretty much all day, every day. Most importantly, I wasn't trying to force it. I invested in self-love because I was not working so hard to make it happen. I took inspired actions that opened up doors bigger than I could have imagined.

Using LOA to attract my financial freedom was easy and it felt good. In fact, it felt like everything just magically happened. And it did. I manifested the house that allowed me to quit my job less than two months after I intended it. I set the intention to find a one-bedroom I could buy and rent out for enough to cover a two-bedroom place for myself. After a weekend fully invested in self-love, I was inspired to talk to my sister about purchasing a place together that met both of our needs. This was something we had never considered before. Within two weeks we were under contract on the perfect place for both of us. It had the three bedrooms and yard she was looking for, and a separate place with two bedrooms for me to live in, and a one-bedroom carriage house that I could rent to cover my half of the mortgage payment. Magic!

If financial freedom, which kind of sounds big and hard, was so easy to manifest, why couldn't I manifest the coaching practice I wanted? For starters, when I really paused to reflect on it, I did not actually *want* a coaching practice. Especially not the coaching practice that I was trying to manifest. I didn't want a practice full of clients. I wanted freedom, and 20 clients a week does not sound like freedom to me.

I'd thought I wanted a coaching practice that had 20 clients a week, because I thought I could make money and not have to go to work that way. What I really wanted was to not have to go to work every day. I did want to be a coach, but that wasn't my first priority. I was just doing it because I thought it was the only way I could make the money I needed to get out of my job.

It is *so* much easier to manifest what you actually want as opposed to the compromise you *think* is going to get you what you want. Have you ever tried it? Think of something you worked really hard to manifest. Did you really want it? Or did you think it would lead to something else?

I was also trying to get away from something (my job) instead of moving toward something. Manifesting away from something rarely leads to creating what you desire. You create more of what you are focused on. Remember how I said it became clear my job was not going to be flexible at all with me building my business? I created that. I was focused on building my business so that I did not have to "work." I wanted freedom, but I was focused on "not working." I got what I was focused on, which was work. I got more limitations on my time and less freedom. I also got more and more work. The Law of Attraction was working. It just was not working the way I thought it would. I hear stories like this in my practice all the time. Someone quits one thing to "get away" from something and they end up creating more of what they're trying to "get away" from. Have you ever thought you were using the Law of Attraction to get what you wanted, but instead created more of what you did not want?

Trying to manifest *getting away from* something causes more stress and more of whatever you are trying to get away from. That is the way it works. The Law of Attraction does not work to solve your problems, because when you are focusing on the problem you will get more of that. You also activate all the feelings you do not want, like fear, stress, desperation. Think about it: If something is chasing you and you are trying to get away, how do you feel? Scared. Panicked. Desperate. Now think about seeing an old friend after you have not seen them in awhile. You are drawn to run to them and get there as fast as you can to embrace them. How does that feel? Inspired. Joyful. Fun.

You feel pulled to your friend. The same thing happens to your energy when you are manifesting. If you are manifesting away from something, you tend to be scared and desperate. When you are manifesting toward something you tend to be inspired and joyful. What energy do you think will attract what you want easier and faster?

I was trying to manifest something to get to something else. Instead of just going for what I wanted, my soul mate, I was trying to manifest a coaching practice, because I thought *not* having one was blocking him from entering my life. Clearly, that wasn't necessarily true. It's hard to manifest something to get to something else. It never works. Even if you get the result you are seeking, you will not feel joyful, because what you get is not what you truly wanted. Actually feeling joy is essential to attracting anything joyful into your life. Like the thing your "how" was supposed to enable. Even if I had manifested 20 people in my coaching practice, I would not have enjoyed it, and that miserable energy would not have attracted my soul mate. Have you tried to manifest something because you thought it would get you something else? Did you get it? If you did, did it feel good?

In the middle of this whole thing, probably right before I threw my hands up, I hired a relationship coach. I knew trying to build my business wasn't working to attract the love of my life. Looking back on it, hiring her to help with the relationship stuff probably allowed me to let go of the version of my coaching practice that I was building and being frustrated by. She didn't say, and we didn't focus on, the idea that I had been building my practice to attract him, but the work we did sure opened up a lot of space. Thank goodness, because that space is what led to a dream come true.

Why else was it easier to manifest financial freedom? I had a clear picture. I said above that I'd wanted 20 clients in my practice, but I'm not sure I even had a clear picture of what I wanted that practice to look like or feel like. Manifesting works best when you can get a clear picture, visual and emotional. I always say the magic is in the details. At any moment, I could jump into the vision of what it would be like to not have to go to work every day. I could make that feel real, in detail, enough to *attract like*.

With financial freedom, I could activate the feeling. It was easy to tap into. I loved how seeing myself financially free felt. I loved how it felt when I added up the numbers. I activated that feeling a lot! It was actually easier to see my financial freedom with my imagination than it was to see a full coaching practice and all its activities.

Have you ever tried to manifest what seemed like the easier thing? Even now, logically, it seems like it would be easier to manifest 20 clients a week then financial independence. But even as I write, I can feel the difference. I am very unlikely to manifest 20 one-on-one clients, because even writing about it doesn't feel good to me. Writing about financial independence brings a smile to my face, every time. So does thinking about having 50 people in my Champagne Life Coaching Group. That lights me up! Again, it's going to be much easier to manifest 50 people to my group coaching than it would be if I set out today to get 20 one-on-one clients. That isn't necessarily intuitive. Yet 50 in group coaching just *feels* better, which means I have a greater chance of attracting that to me. What feels better will always manifest easier than what logically seems like it would be easier to manifest.

I manifested financial independence because I knew the story. I knew how it started, I designed the middle, and envisioned how it would end. I knew the details inside and out. It was a story I told myself and others, over and over again. It was a story that was clear. I never wrote it down, but I internalized it. I spoke it. I thought it. I visualized it. I became the person living it, and then it played out as my story. It was easy to act *as if*, and follow inspiration, from the place of deeply knowing the story I wanted to live.

Did you see yourself in parts of my story? You have the vision board, you have set your intentions, and yet it's not working. Maybe you have found every limiting belief known to humanity, or at least every negative thought you ever think, but you still cannot figure out what is blocking what you desire. When it's not working, do you find yourself working harder? Sign up for another class, read another book, or attend another workshop? Is it feeling like effort and force? Maybe you are trying to manifest something you do not really want. Is it possible you are trying to manifest something to get to something else? In any event, you're not feeling the ease, joy, and lightness you want to experience, and it's causing you to lose hope.

All of that is about to change.

YOU ARE WORTHY OF LIVING THE BEST STORY YOU CAN TELL

How do you create your Champagne Life? You create the ultimate vision (story) of what you desire and you start moving toward that instead of away from your problems. The more you try and fix a "problem," the more problems there are going to be. Can you imagine a life without your current problem or problems? What would it be like if they were just gone? How would your life look and feel?

The best way to get to that place is to dive in, head first, and create the story that you are dreaming of living. Having a story scripted out that you want to be living is the single most powerful Law of Attraction tool you can utilize. Why? Because clarity is the strongest signal you can send out to the Universe. Clarity also tells your own brain what you are doing, which means it can help forge the path.

I am not just talking any story though. I am talking about a story that details every single thing about your Champagne Life Days (ideal days). The magic is in the details. The reason you keep living the same story over and over again is that you do not know another one. Your brain does not have another one to direct you towards. Your brain formulates your current reality based on memory. If the only memories in there are of struggle, failure, and frustration, you are going to continue to experience that because your brain will continue to help you recreate the same stories over and over again based on past experiences.

Think of it like a road trip. Your story is your GPS destination. Recently, you have just been jumping in your car (let's say you're in Denver). You jump in your car and you think to yourself, "I'd like some oranges." So you start driving toward Florida. Except you do not put your destination in the GPS, you just start heading southeast. About the time you hit Arkansas you decide it's taking too long to get to Florida. So you turn around. Meanwhile, it's hot, so you decide you'd like to go somewhere rainy so you point the car toward Seattle. Only—you guessed it—before you even get past Denver, you decide it would be easier if you wanted turquoise jewelry, so you head toward New Mexico. You end up driving around a lot and not really getting anywhere.

This is how a lot of people's manifesting practice goes. If you had stopped and thought about what you really wanted to experience, you could have come up with a destination or two that you wanted to experience and drove right there. Two things from the road trip story tend to happen all the time when people are trying to manifest: You didn't know where you were going, and you decided it was taking too long to get there. You changed your mind. Once you changed your mind, you got even more impatient and decided to go for something easier. You never stopped and thought about what you really wanted to experience. You could have come up with a destination that you wanted to experience and drove right toward it. Do you know anyone who has had this experience before?

How can writing your Champagne Life Story help? First, it's going to give you a GPS point that is so clear and full of details that it draws you to it, rather than you chasing it. You create the details of the life you want to be living rather than just thinking you want to manifest one thing at a time. That is important because it's going to create flow and continuity in your experience of the LOA tools you are working with. It's also going to give you more opportunity to see success.

When you know your Champagne Life Story, you can begin to become the person living that story. The Law of Attraction works. Like attracts like. In order for you to attract your Champagne Life, you have to become the person who would be living that life. It's hard to become that person when you do not have a clear picture of what that life looks like, up close and from the perspective of a first-person experience. You have to know the script.

Scripting out your Champagne Life Story in detail gives you clarity on who you are going to become. It also gives you clarity about what that life is going to look like. It's common for me to hear people say, "I want my business to be successful." *Successful*, like many other words, isn't a definition. There is no clarity in "successful." You are the one who has to clarify what it looks like. Running around chasing an undefined notion of *successful*, literally or via manifesting, is exhausting. It's like taking a route to New Mexico that involves going toward Florida and then Seattle.

Before we talk about how you script your Champagne Life Story, it's important to clarify the difference between a detailed story of the life you desire to live, and controlling the how. I talked to a client recently who wants to be on stage and have a full coaching practice. That's awesome. However, as we started to talk about what she was doing in her business it became evident that the picture is not crystal clear.

How did I know that? She was doing what I call "controlling the how." This is a common mistake people make when they are trying to manifest. She was *wanting* to have a radio show because she thought that would bring more people to her blog, which would get more people commenting on her blog, which would lead to more clients. What she really wanted was more clients and to be on stage. However, she did not know exactly what that looked like so she was trying to put all these pieces together to "make it happen," without a clear picture to move towards.

I understand. I have done it. I successfully used my LOA magic to get my first radio interview on a very popular show that was syndicated in 9 major markets. Do you know how many book sales I got from that interview? One—that's it. And I didn't get anything else from it. Not another interview or a magazine editor contacting me. Just one book sale.

Ok, I got the experience, which was really cool, and I still have the recording of that interview (from 2009) that I put on my site from time to time. I have a great story. I definitely attribute getting on that show to setting the intention and visualizing what I wanted. I got myself lined up for that experience, and I know it happened because of the LOA work I did because I know someone else who didn't get on the show who was hoping to be chosen.

While that experience goes down in history as one of the coolest things I've manifested to date, it is only that: a cool experience I manifested. After buying the one envelope and paying the postage on the book, I made about $10. That is not what I wanted from that experience. I had it backwards. I was manifesting the things I thought would get me what I wanted instead of getting clear first, focusing on what I truly wanted, and letting it manifest. I was manifesting the how. I focused on getting on the radio, when I should have focused on what I actually wanted: clients. Then, if I was inspired to apply for the show, or even had a radio producer contact me, I would have been more successful.

At that point, had I understood what I do now, I would have gotten really clear on what I wanted and I would have let inspiration lead the way. I may not have pursued the radio show at all. There is a difference between following inspiration and doing things because you "think" they are going to work. Inspiration pulls you. It leads you to the exact person and moment you need. Doing things because you think they will work leads to you try doing one thing after another. Inspiration leads you to where you desire to be.

How do you find that inspiration? You don't. It finds you when you get really clear about what it is you desire to create. This is the step most people miss. The first time I got really clear about what I wanted, financial freedom, I was literally lead by inspiration to check out different things and inspired by random ideas that together put me on the fast track to what I desired.

The second time I got really clear about what I wanted and learned to follow my inspiration was when I created the Manifest 10K course (formerly Money, Money, Money). I spent hours scripting, writing the experience as if it had already happened–the success I was going to experience, the people who would show up to sign up. I scripted the number of people. I described how it would feel when they registered. I wrote about the emails they would send me. I wrote about the money I would make. I knew who I was in the process and I knew exactly what I wanted to experience.

The story played out pretty much like I had scripted it and it was a huge success, even though it did not look like it was going to work. I remember scripting, "There are now 170 people enrolled" and, "The sign-ups just keep coming, one after another." I scripted those sentences over a month prior to the start of the course. Just 4 days before the course started I only had 7 people enrolled. That's a far off number from 170. Have you been in a similar situation? Would you have let go of your intention of 170 people? Would you have decided it wouldn't work?

So many people make the decision that it won't work, when it looks like it's not working. And then they start telling themselves it didn't work. Then they get to see evidence of that, too, because that is what they are focused on. And then they give up, and they start to think, *Maybe the Law of Attraction won't work for me.* Have you ever found yourself in that situation? Or thinking, *I just can't figure out how to do it right.*

I chose a different route. I knew it would work, so I just keep moving forward. I tapped into the story that it was working and allowed inspiration to lead the way. Then it happened. I shared a post, following inspiration, about the program on Facebook and someone I knew, who I assumed would have seen the post 5 times already, but hadn't, saw it. She immediately shared it with her tribe on Facebook. Then the sign-ups just started coming, "one after another." I could hardly keep up with how fast they were coming. I responded to each person individually to thank them for registering. And they just kept coming.

I emailed the person who had shared that post on Facebook and said, "Thank you. They just keep coming and coming." Her response, "Oh yeah? Watch this–I'm about to send it out in my newsletter, too." And they just kept coming, "one after another" until there were 170. By the first day of the course there were close to 200 people registered.

Since then, people have sent me emails telling me how awesome the course is. I get money in my in-box all the time. And that program has been named Best LOA Program two years in a row because so many people rave about it.

What if I had given up when I only had 7 people registered? What if I had decided all the work I had done didn't work and I quit trying? You probably wouldn't be reading this book right now.

I see it all the time. People decide it's not working and they go try something else, usually another program. They continue to search for something else that will work. They abandon all the work they have put in and they tell themselves, "That isn't going to work." What if they had stayed the course for one more day and gotten exactly what they wanted? Have you ever decided it wasn't going to work after all? Was it something you really wanted, or were you only telling yourself you wanted it? Were you open to how your intention would manifest, or were you trying to control the how?

Do you think it would have made a difference if you had had a really clear story that detailed what you wanted and you could, for the moments you were in that story, feel it happening? That is the magic of Scripting Your Champagne Life Story. It lets you be in on the experience before it actually happens. I was so in on the experience of my success with Money, Money, Money that I knew it would work. To be honest, there was never a moment I thought about saying, "This isn't going to work," because that wasn't possible. I had already experienced my success in great detail. I knew exactly what it felt like.

This is much the same way one of my clients experienced it. We wrote her Champagne Life Story from a Monday to a Wednesday. When we finished on Wednesday she felt inspired to send out her newsletter and to say a couple things about her year-long program. Within 24 hours she had six new people registered for that program and was experiencing her first four-figure day in business. She was elated. She also knew, from scripting, what the experience of success felt like. It happened automatically.

She was inspired to send another email a few days later to people she knew had seen the offer, and had another person register through a link without even talking to her. She knows what success feels like. She also knows how to tap into that successful person, her Champagne Self, who is already living her dream life and knows how to harness that toward knowing what to do next. Just 10 days after we completed her Champagne Life Story, she sold out her coaching program.

Just so you do not think my client is special and was already rocking her business, let me tell you that she was struggling. She wanted to make more money. She is amazing at what she does. She just couldn't figure out how to get people into her program. By her own admission, she was frustrated and in some ways ready to give-up. She didn't start out on top of the world, but after three days of clarifying her story and helping her step into it, she emerged a different person. She was the person who would be living her successful outcome. She learned that the person you want to be is already here and you can access her anytime. That makes all the difference.

You are worthy of living the best story you can tell. You are worthy of living the dream that you have been too afraid to admit. You are worth living a story that is easier and that feels better. You are worthy of living your Champagne Life Story.

LEARN MORE ABOUT PUTTING THESE PRINCIPLES INTO ACTION

LISTEN TO *Manifest it Now* ON ITUNES

HOW TO CREATE YOUR CHAMPAGNE LIFE STORY

You have read that when I was launching my first big program I scripted a lot. Scripting your Champagne Life Story is like writing a regular script, but a lot more intense and a lot more detailed. One of the reasons I was so successful is that scripting out the details of how I wanted that launch and that program to go became as much a part of creating the program as writing the actual program. I visited a friend in the middle of writing and she remembers me taking every moment we were not engaged in conversation to open my laptop and write the course and the story of how it would go.

I would script something about the success of the course before I would start writing the course for the day. Then if I got stuck and didn't know what to write, I would go back to scripting the success of course. When it came time to write the sales copy (which was a blog post, by the way) I wrote more about how successful the course was and what that experience felt like to me. I wrote *a lot* about the successful experience of that course in the 6 weeks I spent writing the material and the assets to support the course itself.

The concentrated focus on scripting the success of the course is one of the reasons I believe it was successful. I got to know the course as a success, from the very beginning, and I also got to experience myself as a successful leader through scripting out the experience.

Earlier this year, I wrote my second book, *Investing Secrets for a Champagne Life*. The book is about investing in real estate. Prior to writing it I had said I wouldn't buy and sell real estate this year. That seemed like a fact, because I did not think I had anything else that I could buy and sell.

I wrote that book in three days. Within six weeks of publishing that book, I was under contract to buy two houses and sell one. Since then, I have revamped my whole real estate strategy and plan on selling all my Denver properties and buying less expensive properties in other markets. When all is said and done with my real estate plan, I will have increased my monthly income by 67% from my investments.

I attribute this huge shift in my plans for the better to two things. The first is my daily amping up of my money vibe. The second is that I wrote a book about real estate investing in three days. In those three days, over about 18 hours, in fact, my sole focus was on the magic of real estate. I was reliving deals. I was writing all about my success. I was illustrating great returns on investments. I was talking about how much the value of my properties had increased. I was fully immersed in telling the story of how successful I am at real estate investing. And that story started coming true even more within six weeks of writing that book, without me consciously doing anything new. I felt myself guided and led to check out things, evaluate things, ask questions, and–voila, like magic, I had a new real estate plan.

That is how I learned the power of scripting your Champagne Life Story very intensely in a short amount of time. I did not intend to have all that real estate stuff unfold. In fact, I really did think there was no reason or possibility to be doing any real estate deals this year. It hadn't been my focus, but now that it is done, the success of that new strategy is delivering the means to achieve outcomes that I had intended to manifest, too.

I am going to walk you through the steps to creating your Champagne Life Story as best I can. The first thing I would do is read this book all the way through. Then set aside time to script your Champagne Life Story. I would suggest setting aside 16 hours over 3 days. You can do it however you like, but 16 hours over 3 days is going to yield the best results. The concentration of time inside your story makes a huge difference for a number of reasons.

The first reason is that you are focused mostly on your story, so worry and doubt are less likely to creep in. You are focusing all your information on the positive outcome you desire. That focus does not leave room for negative stuff, second-guessing, procrastination, or any of the things that so often get in our way without clear and consistent focus.

The second reason is that your brain starts to change in three days. Spending three days focusing on this stuff is literally going to change your brain to support your new story. If you know anything about your brain, you know it is powerful. Its job is to keep you safe. And it likes details, or else it fills in the blank. As you fill in the details you are keeping your brain from filling in details with past experiences that might not be helpful to your future goals.

During this process you are also painting for the Universe a very clear picture of what you desire. The magic is in the details. Giving the Universe very clear instructions about the life you desire to create makes it more likely you will get that life, because your energy, your behavior, your actions, and your awareness of opportunities are all headed toward the same place. Putting all the detailed information out there in a short time and in a concentrated way makes it more likely you will get what you desire faster and easier, because you are experiencing it in depth as you are scripting it.

Take a moment and look at your calendar. If you are serious about creating a Champagne Life, pick three days in a row that you can focus on scripting your new story. Schedule the time on your calendar right now. If you are reading this and thinking to yourself, I'm in... but I don't want to do it on my own. I want the support of someone who can help me do it click here (http://www.liveyourchampagnelife.com/script-your-champagne-life-workshop) to join the next workshop. You can do it on your own and I am going to set you up for as much success as I can, but I am the type of person who does better with support and being lead through something new, and you may be, too, so know that my help is available as well.

PREPARATION-GATHERING THE PIECES

Your Champagne Life Story starts with your Champagne Days. If you have ever heard of an Ideal Day exercise, that is very similar to a Champagne Day. Your Champagne Days are days that at the end of them you want to sit and just breath in all the awesomeness. You want to toast your entire day. These are the days that are filled with everything you love about your life. They are filled with your dearest experiences and complimented by the most wonderful people you can imagine. Your ideal days flow from one joyous thing to another. They are days that when they are over you want to pinch yourself to make sure they are real.

I believe we have more than one Champagne Day. I believe three is the magic number. This comes from working with many clients on their ideal days. I used to create visualizations based on my clients' Champagne Days. What I found through interviewing my clients is that everything they desire usually fits nicely into three Champagne Days that encompass everything wanted in their dream life. Often, one day will be a typical day that is filled with everyday things that feel really good. The second is usually about a trip or a more atypical day. The third is usually something big, maybe something big for the business or planning a trip or a relaxation day in the middle of the week.

For my client, Jill, there were very distinct days that represented how she wanted her life to look. The first day involved being in a city, going for a run in an amazing park, and working with the energy of the city surrounding her. Her second day revolved around being in Europe on an amazing vacation with a girlfriend. Her third Champagne Day was running a retreat for her business. Your Champagne Days will naturally evolve out of the next exercises.

How do you figure out what your days might be?

Take out a sheet of paper. Write down everything you want to experience in your Champagne Life. Rather than put it in a list format, write all over the paper, like you would in a brainstorming session. Set a timer for five minutes and just write down as many things as you can think of. Allow what comes up to come up. Don't analyze it or question it. Just write it down and let one idea inspire another. There is also a list of questions in the Champagne Life Toolkit that can help you add to your experience list. You can download it here (http://www.liveyourchampagnelife.com/life-style-design-toolkit).

Keep writing until you feel like you've come to a natural stopping place. When you come to a natural stop, look at your list. Notice if there are any themes. Start to notice what things would fit together on the same day. What activities would naturally flow together on what days? Take different color highlighters and mark what activity goes with what day.

After you have color-coded your days, see if there is anything that did not naturally fit into a day. Those things can be sprinkled into your three days. For example, if one of your days isn't about being on a trip, but travel is part of your Champagne Life, you can script in how you purchased tickets and made reservations at an amazing hotel during one of your three days. You are going to use all the good stuff you have written down to script your Champagne Life Days.

Now, check to see that everything you have written down is what you desire. If you have something that you do not want, cross it out. Think about what would replace that and script it in. For example, maybe you wrote, "Pay off debt," but need to cross that off and put what you want instead, which is likely more than enough money to do the things you enjoy. If there is anything you want to change or get rid of in your life right now, ask yourself what you want instead. What would your life be like in the absence of that problem you are thinking about? Imagine how it would feel? What are you going to do with the time that you are currently spending thinking about and interacting with that current problem? Write down how you will be spending that time and energy in your Champagne Days, because that "problem" is not a part of your Champagne Life.

Look at the page filled with what is going to happen during your Champagne Days. How are you going to feel inside that those days, living that life? Write that down. Think about how you feel about yourself when you are living that life, and write it down. Think about any current thoughts or feelings you have about yourself that you no longer want to participate in. Write them down. Then cross them out and replace them with how you do want to think and feel about yourself. You will sprinkle these details into your Champagne Days as well. For example, if you will love the way your body looks in your Champagne Days, you can write something like, "On my way out of the bedroom I pass the mirror and I think, you look amazing!" Or, if you do not want to feel anxious in your Champagne Life, you can sprinkle in something like, "I am calm and feel peaceful." Make note of the things you want to sprinkle into your Champagne Life Days.

Did you include the sacred parts of your day? Yoga, meditation, playing with your dog, etc. Are you working in your Champagne Life Story? If so, how many hours a day are you working? What are you doing? Ask yourself if there is anything else you need to add?

SCRIPTING YOUR CHAMPAGNE LIFE DAYS

Now that you have all the parts of your days, it is time to script the first of your Champagne Life Days. Pick a day, any day to begin with. You are going to script out your experience of your day from the time you wake up to the time you lay your head on your pillow.

The best place to think about in terms of what point in time you are scripting is five years out. You can do it closer in as long as it feels really good.

Have you ever been in a workshop or read a book that gave you a similar exercise, to script it out as if it happened, when you did that it felt flat? You felt like you must have done something wrong. There was no juice, and you saw no results in the weeks to months following. I understand. I have had that same experience before. This is going to be different. I promise.

I am going to give you my magic formula to make your ideal day come to life in your mind. The first thing to think about when you are doing this is you want it to be as long as possible. Ideally, your Champagne Day will take you close to two hours to script and will be close to 2,000 words. Take a deep breath. I know that sounds like a lot. I am going to walk you through it.

Start by setting the timer for an hour. As you sit down to create and script, think about yourself as the on-the-spot reporter rather than the news anchor who reads the news from the professional environment of the news room. An example: You are watching the news and the newsroom reporter says, "The hurricane has brought 80 MPH winds and lots of rain to the city. But the on-the-spot reporter is attempting to stand out there in the 80 mile an hour winds and talk about the experience. They are getting soaked by the rain. Their hair is a mess. They are focused on how it feels to be there, how they can barely stand up. That the rain just keeps coming. They are describing the umbrella that got turned inside out. They are describing to you how hard it is to walk into the direction of the driving rain. They describe what it was like to feel the calm of the eye and then to feel the storm again. They relay to you how they felt. For years to come, they will be telling a different story about that hurricane than the newsroom reporter.

When you are writing your Champagne Days, script them from the perspective of the on-the-spot reporter. Report how things feel both physically and emotionally. Report what you are thinking. Report how appreciative you are for the moments you are living. Include what surprises you. Be as in-the-moment as you can. Here are two examples:

NEWSROOM REPORTER STYLE

I woke up this morning, and got ready. I went to have break-
fast. I had eggs and toast. Then I went for a run. After my run
I showered and got ready. Then I went to my computer and
started working. I answered client emails. I checked my bank
accounts and there was a lot of money in there. I called a client
and then I took a break for lunch.

ON-THE-SPOT REPORTER STYLE

I opened my eyes when the sun began hitting my face through
my bedroom window. I stretched a little before opening my
eyes to the most beautiful view outside my window. I laid
there and enjoyed the beauty of the mountains. The snow is
almost gone, but they are still beautifully white at the top.
When I was ready I sat up and smiled. My feet hit the beau-
tiful rug next to my bed and I headed off to do my morning
routine. The first thing I did was hit the start button on the
coffee. As the smell of freshly brewed coffee started to fill my
kitchen I scrambled some eggs with feta and spread the jelly
I got at the farmer's market on top of my toast. I sat down to
enjoy my breakfast. I sat outside on the deck where the birds
were chirping and you could hear everyone getting up and
getting going.

After breakfast, I grabbed my new running shoes and headed
out for a run. The morning air was still crisp, just the way I

like it. I passed the old house that I love and ran down my favorite tree-lined street. The leaves were bright green and shaded me from the sun that was getting further and further up into the sky.

I returned home sweaty, tired, and exhilarated all at the same time. I took a shower and was ready to start my day. I went to my computer and opened it up. There were two emails from clients telling me how amazing their lives have become since working with me.

After replying to their wonderful emails I opened up my bank account online and—holy moly—there is a lot of money in there. I knew this was a good month but I guess I didn't realize how good it was. I transferred some money to my savings account. It's time to figure out where to move the large sum of money in the savings account to. I sent my investment broker an email so we can discuss what to invest the money in. Next up I had a call with a client I love. We had a great session. They experienced some major shifts and breakthroughs in that one hour. I could feel my stomach grumbling so I knew it was time to take a break from lunch.

The on-the-spot experience was better right? Did you feel like you were more into the story? Could you see the story in your mind better than you could when I was reporting from the newsroom desk? Being the on-the-spot reporter in your own story makes you feel more like you are in the experience of it.

Now we're going to take it even further. The biggest mistake I see people make when they are doing something like this is not connecting enough to the feelings. One of the reasons you are doing this is to *actually get to know* the person you are becoming. Your brain likes to know the details. Your brain wants to know you can make the change and be ok. Your brain wants to know how you are going to feel and how you are going to react.

Additionally, your brain bases your experience of reality on your memories. By writing in past tense, as if you are at the end of your day looking back, you are creating a pseudo memory that your brain can now recall in the present and the future to create experiences similar to your ideal days. The more emotion you add to your script, the more magic the memory will have.

When I started this very detailed, emotionally rich, textured method of scripting, I was working on my story about being in a relationship with my soulmate. I had been scripting for awhile. It would go something like this...

I absolutely love the man I am with. He is amazing. We have so much fun together. I love how good of a man he is. He makes me laugh. We have a great time together.

Then I realized I needed to have a clearer picture of the experience. What I was doing was great, but I wasn't getting to know myself in the context of the situation or relationship I was seeking. I decided I needed the details. That is when I started scripting out the whole day. What we did. How we interacted. What he said to me. How I responded to him. I have been single a long time and I needed to know what that would be like to be with someone else–with my ideal man, my soulmate–in a committed relationship. I started scripting in more detail.

You are equal parts getting familiar with your story and getting familiar with you, as you will become, by the actual living of that story. One place I see this go really wrong for people is that they just keep listing things that happen in their Champagne Day and they are not emotionally connected to the story. Experiencing the emotions in the story, experiencing the full sensory detail in your envisioning makes it more real. It connects you into it. It draws you into the experience and that is what starts to change your brain.

The more you add how it feels into your story, the better your story will be. The more you will feel like you are in it. The more familiar you will become with who you are inside your future story. Then, when your brain searches for "memories," it will have these stories that you are now familiar with in the mix to choose from. Your story will come true quicker and easier. There is a formula for getting completely emotionally and sensorily immersed in your story.

Before I share the formula, take five minutes and script part of one of your Champagne Days.

Now that you know what it feels like, I will introduce my formula for getting deeper and deeper into the your story emotionally and also being able to see it and feel it more.

<u>Detail + Sense + Feeling + Gratitude/Appreciation</u>

Detail: Add a very specific detail through on-the-spot-reporting.

Example: I woke up.

Sense: Describe how one or more of your senses (sight, hearing, touch, smell, taste) is activated.

Example: I felt the warmth of the sun on my face.

Feeling: Describe the emotions or feelings you are experiencing in the story.

Example: I feel so happy. I am so excited.

Gratitude/Appreciation: State your gratitude and/or appreciation.

Example: I am so grateful I get to wake up when my body is ready and naturally awakens.

Here is an example:

I awoke (detail) to the warmth of the sun on my face (sense) this morning. I was so happy (emotion) as I put my feet on the floor, because I was excited (emotion) to get up and start an amazing day. I am so grateful (gratitude/appreciation) that I get to wake up every morning with the sun and I get to get up and do what I want before starting my work day.

I smiled as I walked down the hall (detail). The smell (sense) of coffee brewing lured me to the kitchen. I felt a deep sense of joy (feeling) as I entered and saw the man responsible for the wonderful smell. I said to him, "I appreciate you." (appreciation) and kissed him on the cheek before pouring myself a cup of coffee and sitting next to him.

* * *

Can you feel the difference? Do you feel more a part of the story? Can you feel your senses and emotions being activated?

Take a minute to read over what you wrote before. On a scale of 1-10, how connected do you feel to what you wrote? Go back and apply the magic formula to it and rescript it. Then read it and see how it feels. Rate it on a scale of 1-10 for how connected you feel.

The magic is in the details of the emotion and your senses.

Set aside two hours to script each of your Champagne Life Days. Now that you know the formula it is going to be a lot easier. If you script your days with enough emotion and detail they should feel like a good book you do not want to put down. In this case, you will not want to stop writing. They should feel like a story that draws you in. If you do not get that feeling, go back and make sure you are following the formula. Add in more emotion, describe how your senses are being activated, and add gratitude and appreciation.

SPEAK YOUR CHAMPAGNE LIFE STORY

Speaking your Champagne Life Story into existence is the next step. Verbal scripting is so powerful. You know words are powerful. You create what you speak. When you speak, the Universe hears on a whole different level. You also hear yourself on a whole new level.

Right after I quit my job, I went speed dating. I said out loud over and over again, "I'm a life coach." I had been a life coach for years, but I would always say, "I have a life coaching business on the side." For the first time, I spoke the story about being a life coach full-time. I said it more than twenty times that night and afterward I felt different. I owned the story that I was speaking, that I am a life coach.

In the same way you are getting familiar with what your Champagne Life picture looks and feels like when you are writing, when you speak you are hearing yourself "be" the person in your Champagne Life. You are also experiencing the language of your Champagne Life. It is different than the language you are speaking now, and it's important to hear it and to hear yourself speak from inside of your Champagne Life.

Verbal scripting is a very important step in integrating your new story. I have been using this technique with a friend for years. We get on the phone as if we are right in the middle of what we want and we talk about it. Magical "ah-has" and breakthroughs have happened in those moments. It also paved the way for us to walk right into our stories, because we knew how they sounded, how they felt, and their details. You worked out most of the details when you wrote your Champagne Days.

During the Script Your Champagne Life Workshop, we do this as an interview. With my client Jill, I took her to the end of one of her Champagne Days (the end of a fabulous retreat she had just put on), had her imagine everything around her, and then I played the role of an interviewer from a popular running magazine.

I asked her about the retreat. I asked her why she created it. I asked her how it all came together. I asked her what, if anything, she had had to get over to get to this point in her life. I asked her why people join her group. Because she had already fleshed out most of the details, telling her story was easy. In the moments it wasn't right on the tip of her tongue, I told her to take a deep breath and let the answer come. It always did. It always does.

Being in the interview space–talking about the details of her Champagne Life–magically transformed her into the version of herself that will be living that life. She found pieces of herself she hadn't discovered yet, and was able to see the answers to some of the challenges she has been having. The answers came easily. She heard herself speak as a different person. She was able to get to know her future self so she could tap into her anytime she needed to.

The difference between the process in this book and what I have done with my friend in the past is that you know the details, so the story flows very easily. You already know the answers. You just have to give them a little time to bubble up. What you are really doing is giving your future self a chance to come into the present.

After our interview, Jill had the answers she needed to move forward in her business. She knew she had the answers people wanted. Speaking her script gave her a chance to hear and see her own answers, the answers she had been struggling to find for months. There is magic in this process that will make your life so much easier and get you what you want even quicker.

Your next step is to do an interview. If you have a friend who can play along, ask them. If you do not have a friend or significant other who can play along and hold the space, I invite you to ask your coach. If you cannot find anyone who is ready, willing, and able to play along, talk to yourself. It's ok. It is totally worth it.

Put yourself at the end of one of your Champagne Days. Imagine being there. In this moment, who would want to interview you? Think of a magazine or a TV show, or maybe Oprah. What would they want to know? Write that down.

Some questions might be:

- *Describe a typical day in your life.*

- *How did you get here, to this moment?*

- *Why did you create what you created?*

- *What was the biggest obstacle you had to overcome?*

- *What do you consider to be your greatest success?*

- *What would you tell your younger self?*

- *If you had this journey to do over again, would you do it?*

- *What is the biggest lesson you have learned along the way?*

- *What advice would you give someone just starting out?*

DESCRIBE A TYPICAL DAY IN YOUR LIFE

If you have someone to play with you, give them the questions and speak these answers out loud. This gives your answers more energy and makes them even more likely to come true. Take a minute to read your Champagne Life Day and then have them interview you. If you do not have someone who will do it with you, imagine you do and answer the questions out loud. It is very important that you answer them out loud. The voice you are most susceptible to is your own. If you say it, it's true. It is a good idea to record the interview and listen to it daily.

SCRIPT YOUR CHAMPAGNE LIFE STORY

At this point you have a very clear picture of the destination. You have created your Champagne Days and you have spoken as the new version of yourself. Now that you are really familiar with that person at the destination, that amazing version of yourself, it's time to fill in the blanks. The reason you keep living the same story over and over again is because it is the only one you know. It is time to create a new story that leads you to your desired destination. The great news is you now have a very clear picture of your desired destination.

You are literally going to fill in the script of what happens between now and then. At this point, you have likely experienced some "ah-has." You have probably also had some inspiring ideas surface. Use the questions and prompts below to script your complete new story.

- *First line: I love my life.* Describe your life now (as if you are living all your Champagne Days).

- *Line: It wasn't always like this.* Describe where you were when you started this process. How were you feeling? Were you frustrated?

- What changed? What prompted the shift? What set you on the path to your Champagne Days? (This might be reading this book and actually doing the process. It could be a culmination of things that all happened around the same time.)

- What did you have to overcome? What challenges did you face along the way to your Champagne Days?

- What adjustments did you make along the way?

- What was your greatest fear?

- What actions did you take? What was the bridge between then (when you started your story) and now (the place where you are living your Champagne Days)?

- What is the best part of your Champagne Life?

- What is the best advice you would give someone who is frustrated with where they are?

* * *

You may want to write to the answers to the questions first and then take them all and script a story, or it might work better for you to just look them over and think about them and sit down and script your story. This process will take you 2–3 hours. As you are going through the questions the answers will surface. You may also be surprised to find that answers will surface that you have been looking for.

Why is this going to work? Scripting your story clearly defines the outcomes and what is going to happen along the way. Your brain now knows how to get past the obstacles, because you've laid them out and written that you got through them.

Including the parts that are true right here and right now, how you were feeling, and what changed, lets your brain and the Universe know this is the story. This is what is going to happen. Scripting the story also lessens any fear your Champagne Days might evoke about being able to make them happen.

One important note is that scripting your story is not about outlining every detail about *how* it happened. You don't need to say that you wrote sixteen blog posts a week and then one got picked up by The Huffington Post and then you were so popular that you were catapulted directly to fame and high demand. You want to leave those details up to the Universe, because it can put together a much better plan than you could ever imagine.

Your story is about loosely describing point A to point B and honoring that there will be some bumps, but that you get through them. Your new story is about having a new storyline to follow. How long have you been living your current story? How long have things really not been moving forward? You need a new storyline to follow and you have just created it. Now you know where you are going. You know where everything is leading. That is magical!

LEARN MORE ABOUT PUTTING THESE PRINCIPLES INTO ACTION

LISTEN TO *Manifest it Now* ON iTUNES

EXPERIENCING YOUR CHAMPAGNE LIFE

CHAMPAGNE LIFE DAYS

The next step is experiencing your Champagne Life. There are many ways to experience your Champagne Life. This will likely require some planning, possibly an investment, and maybe even enlisting some support. Pick the easiest Champagne Life Day to integrate into your current life. Now pick a day on your calendar. You want the day to be as open as possible so that you can completely fill it with your ideal day or days.

Investing your time, energy, and money into an ideal day experience will be one of the most worthwhile investments you will ever make. It may take a little bit of time and saving to create your ideal day, or, like it did for Jill, it might work to do it two days from now.

Jill was transitioning out of one thing into another, so part of her ideal day was to not do anything that resembled her old business. We wanted to fully integrate her into her Champagne Life. Luckily, she had a massage coming up in a few days so we picked that day to become her ideal day. She did everything she could to make it her ideal day, including going to a beautiful park for her run and getting coffee.

We even scheduled me to act like a couple of sale prospects. Part of her Champagne Life Day was making more than one sale in a day. I was going to help her practice that.

We planned it all out, and then the day actually created itself. She was inspired after we completed our work on her story to send out a newsletter. She used the words she was inspired to use, and the next day she had six people enroll in her yearlong program and she experienced her first four-figure day. The energy of what we created was so strong that she lived one of her ideal days the day after we completed our work together. It created itself.

When you invest your time and energy and make commitments to things like practicing your ideal day, the Universe responds. It has to. The Universe is a reflection of you. What you put out there is what you are going to get back. When you spend a concentrated amount of time, energy, and focus on putting something new out there, you get that new experience back.

The more fully you invest in experiencing your Champagne Days, the more you will get to experience them on a daily basis. Experience one of your Champagne Days as soon as you can and then do it as often as you can.

Before I quit my job, I took a week off to "practice" being a coach. I wanted to be familiar with the experience. I set up my week just like a Champagne Life Coaching Day. I scheduled clients, I planned what I was going to do. Later, when I quit my job, stepping into the experience of being a full-time life coach felt a lot easier.

Whenever I am at the beach, I experience one of my Champagne Days by working from the beach. Part of one of my Champagne Days is staying on the beach for an extended period of time. So, instead of just being on vacation when I'm at the beach, for one day I will practice. I practice being there for an extended period of time, which means I'll be working there. So, I work. I set my day up just like I would if I was living there instead of visiting.

Find a way to practice as much of Your Champagne Days as possible. The sooner after creating your new story, the better, because then you will have a tangible experience that goes along with your story. The more you experience your story, the quicker and easier you will draw your desired destination to you.

YOUR CHAMPAGNE LIFE
WARDROBE

What do you look like at your desired destination? What are you wearing? Close your eyes and and let the image come to you. It might be a little or a lot different than what you wear now or how you look, but that difference matters.

Integrate that image into your life now. This could involve buying a new outfit or a new pair of shoes that represents you at your desired destination. Simply hanging that representation of that you in your closet is another reminder to you, your brain, and the Universe that your new story is real. Even if you can't get a new outfit or shoes, shift your closet around. Get rid of the stuff the person living your Champagne Life wouldn't wear. Put the things she or he would wear at the front, easily visible.

YOUR CHAMPAGNE LIFE
VISION BOARD

After completing your Champagne Life Story, create a vision board. Only not your typical vision board. Vision boards are usually what you want. This vision board is going to be a visual representation of what your life looks like from inside your Champagne Life Story. You know your future self really well now. Create a vision board that represents your Champagne Life.

Yes, Pintrest is great and if that is the only way you have to create a vision board, do it that way. You will, however, get more juice out of creating an old-fashioned vision board. Go get yourself some magazines that represent your Champagne Life. Tap into that future version of yourself, the one living your Champagne Life, and go through the magazines as if you are actually shopping with all the money you need. Then create a vision board that is a snapshot of what your Champagne Life looks and feels like.

Visual imprints sent to the Universe are very powerful. Creating your Champagne Life Board and putting it somewhere that you see it frequently is going to greatly increase the visual input that you are putting out into the Field/Universe. You are also going to see this visual representation and be transported into your story for a few moments every time you see it.

In addition to putting it where you can see it, keep your eyes out for elements of it that you can bring into your space to continue drawing your Champagne Life into your current reality. For example, my current Champagne Life Board has a Buddha on it. When I found a Buddha that looked like the one on my vision board, I purchased it and I have it sitting next to my desk, so that I can see that reality is coming true quickly. One of the participants in my Manifest 10K course had a purple vase very similar to one on her vision board show up in the new place she is moving to. This is huge evidence that the reality of that board is coming true and that she is on the right path.

YOUR CHAMPAGNE LIFE HOME

After you finish the process of creating your new story, shift the energy in your home. Clean it, rearrange it, set it up to be a representation of your Champagne Life. Get rid of anything the future you would not have. And bring in things that the future you would have. If you are not sure what to do with something, close your eyes and find your way to your Champagne Life. When you open your eyes, you'll know if what you are looking at belongs in your story or not.

Find as many ways as you can to make your environment match your Champagne Life. Then you are reflecting to the Universe that the story is true and the Universe will have to make it so. My friend Goddess Jacqui is the best person I know at doing this. In fact, I hired her to come help me with a home I was moving into. Within 8 months of us setting up my home as a representation of my Champagne Life, I moved into a new home that is a bigger version of what we created.

One of the things I want to be doing in my Champagne Life is traveling, so we set up my bedroom space to look like a hotel bedroom. We did this very deliberately and inexpensively. There are lots of ways to bring your future into your present. For example, if you want more space, create space. Make sure your place feels spacious and not cramped. Goddess Jacqui and I made my 495-square-foot studio feel very spacious, and now I live in 812-square-foot place that feels so spacious. No matter how small your place is, you can find a way to make your current environment match your Champagne Life.

Another example might be that you want a grand piano in your foyer. Start by clearing the space in your foyer, or creating or allocating a foyer space if you do not already have one. I did not really have a foyer in my previous home, so I used the closest part of the living room to create that feeling that I wanted in a foyer. Ask yourself if there's going to be anything sitting on the grand piano. A book of music, flowers? If the answer is yes, purchase that. If your current space is big enough for the piano, leave space open for where the piano will go. If it's not currently big enough, find a small table that is a similar color and finish to the piano in your Champagne Life. Put it in your foyer, or the space you have created to be your foyer. Place whatever is going to be on the piano on top of the table. Make sure the feeling of the representation matches what it is going to feel like to have a grand piano in your foyer. If you have the space for the piano, don't be surprised if it shows up very quickly. And if you do not yet have the space, do not be surprised if you move to a new place very soon that does have the space.

There are so many ways to create an environment that represents your Champagne Life. The most important step is to identify the feeling of your Champagne Life Story. Then integrate that feeling into your home. If something does not match that feeling, let it go. If something new does match that feeling, keep it or bring it in.

For example, if your future home feels very luxurious bring in as much luxury now as you can. For me, I bought one pillow that was white with gold and silver all over it. That pillow represents my Champagne Life (the next version). Every time I see it I feel abundant. If your carpet is not luxurious but you can't afford to replace it yet, buy a luxurious rug that feels like that luxury. Put it in the middle of your floor so you can experience that feeling as often as possible. Like attracts like, so having that carpet there is likely going to attract the luxurious carpet in your Champagne Life very quickly.

I hire Jaqui to work with the clients in my year-long coaching program because I believe this piece is so important. It's also something that takes practice to learn and understand. It's a skill I have acquired, but it took practice. If you'd like some support with this, I've included a call series Jacqui and I did where we discuss what we did in my former home and how we upleveled my new home. You can get the toolkit here (http://www.liveyourchampagnelife.com/lifestyle-design-toolkit) The more your home looks and feels like your Champagne Life, the quicker you will be living your Champagne Life.

APPRECIATE WHAT ALREADY IS YOUR CHAMPAGNE LIFE

There are going to be parts of your Champagne Life Story and your Champagne Life Days that already exist in your life right now. Start appreciating those parts as much as possible. Appreciation always leads to more. When you shift your focus and appreciation to the things that are part of your Champagne Life, your dream will get to you faster and easier.

Appreciation is one of the reasons I upleveled my home so fast. Jacqui and I set it up to be a gorgeous representation of my Champagne Life. Every time I walked through the front door, I appreciated my home. Instead of focusing on how it was only 495 square feet, I would appreciate how spacious it felt and how I had everything I needed.

I organized the closet so there was a place for everything, which made it feel big. I would appreciate that every time I opened the doors to get something. I integrated the elements I could, like chandeliers, and appreciated the beauty of those. I kept it beautifully clean and organized so that it was easy to appreciate the spacious, luxurious feeling. I made it a point to appreciate every part of my home, especially the parts I could have easily complained about.

The more you appreciate your current life and everything in it, the quicker you will get everything in your Champagne Life. Appreciation amplifies everything and it is the best way to get more of what you want. Start appreciating anything and everything that will be a part of your Champagne Life.

APPRECIATE YOURSELF

Throughout the process of scripting your Champagne Life Story, you are going to discover how amazing you are. Appreciate all those parts of yourself you uncover. Appreciate yourself for taking the time to script your new story and for even having the courage to dream about your Champagne Life. Identify the characteristics that get you to your Champagne Life and appreciate those things about yourself every day.

Here is an exercise to help you appreciate even more about yourself. Get a notebook and a pen. Tap into your Champagne Life. Now write 50 things you appreciate about yourself inside your Champagne Life. Do all 50 at once. Keep listing them until you get to 50. It might take awhile, but this exercise opens up so much appreciation for yourself. After completing this exercise you will have so many things to appreciate about yourself on a daily basis. When you are living your Champagne Life, you are not going to be criticizing yourself for what you are not doing, you are going to be appreciating yourself for what you have done. Start appreciating yourself now. It's a good exercise to do once a week.

LEARN MORE ABOUT PUTTING THESE PRINCIPLES INTO ACTION

LISTEN TO *Manifest it Now* ON ITUNES

WHAT TO DO NEXT

If you have invested the concentrated time and energy I've recommended into creating your Champagne Life Story, you have created an energetic destination. The most important job now is to let that be your lighthouse. That destination is the place that will guide you to it. Whenever you wonder about a decision, instantly check in with the your future self, the one who is living your Champagne Life. That is how you are going to get to that destination faster.

You will learn to follow what you know for sure instead of what you think. This takes practice and is a matter of checking in with your future self and getting the answer. You no longer have to "make this happen." You have already created it. It is happening already. You simply need to create a life that mirrors your Champagne Life as much as possible, and to stay on the path towards that life by following your inspiration. Inspiration is the director of your Champagne Life. It knows the script already, and will lead you to the final scene where you are living your dream.

Inspiration is the quiet whisper that pops an idea into your head out of nowhere. It's the nudge to go this way, when you *think* you should go that way. It can look like getting lost, but actually finding exactly what you are looking for because of the detour. Inspiration is your inner GPS leading you to your dream life.

Inspiration does not yell. It feels like a force pulling you, rather than you pushing you. It is your intuition and signs from the Universe, all rolled into one. Inspiration, if you listen, will lead you down the path that leads to your Champagne Life. Honor it by listening and leaving quiet space for it to be heard. Slow down, so you can hear the quiet whispers that are leading you to exactly where you desire to be.

Fuel your inspiration by doing things that feel inspiring. Give yourself permission to say, "no" to things that do not feel inspired, or in alignment with what you desire. Invest your time and energy in the things you are drawn to, which fill you up and honor who you are. These things are your inspiration, leading you to be more of your Champagne Self. Trust the process.

Write a journal entry every day from your Champagne Life. Fifteen minutes is enough, but do as much as feels good. Doing it in the morning will set you up for success throughout each day. If you want to take it a step further, verbally talk about your story to yourself or to a friend. Act as if you are living it when you are speaking, and get even clearer about what it sounds like.

The good news about this process is that it is it is so powerful. You can let go of most of the other things you are doing. You want to actively engage in journaling from your Champagne Days. Continue to speak your Champagne Days and touch them in any way possible, but you no longer have to work so hard at this LOA thing.

You have done the heavy lifting. There might be things that come up that you either want to engage in or think you would enjoy engaging in and that is wonderful — do it. You can let go of the feeling that you *have* to do this or that, and learn more about this or that so you can get to your ideal life. You do not have to chase the next thing anymore. You get to just be and to practice being your future self as much as possible.

I believe less is more. The less effort required — while your energy is more focused on what you desire — the better. Spend the extra time and energy on integrating as much of your Champagne Life into every day as possible.

You have built the car, your job now is to steer. The first thing you need to do is start an evidence log. Your evidence log is going to be one of your most valuable possessions. Get a new notebook or journal if you want to, or create a new GoogleDoc. You are going to document this stuff.

An evidence log is the place where you keep all the evidence that what you desire, Your Champagne Life, is getting closer and closer to you. I think of it like being a detective. A detective would have all these clues that lead to your Champagne Life, and they would follow them until their objective was fully realized. One of my favorite clients calls the evidence log "proof." I have watched her blossom into possibilities since she started tracking her proof. One of the participants in Manifest 10K refers to her evidence log as "bread crumbs." And another coach I know calls it "reasons to believe," which may sound like a reference to a background in marketing, but it reminds her to stay her course and continue to believe in her destination.

My favorite piece of evidence is actually the engagement of two of my best friends. A few years ago, I was working my magic to draw in my soulmate (he's still not here yet, but I know he's just around the corner). In a lot of my work, I like to get out past what's desired, which is what you do when you script your Champagne Life. Because of this I wasn't working on thinking about "the guy" or "the first date with the guy" I was thinking beyond that. I was working my magic around the proposal, because at the proposal stage he's already here.

I would walk and run down to this place on the river, right in the middle of Denver. There is this one place where I would stop to meditate and to visualize. I would visualize my engagement. I love both intimacy and the being surrounded by those I love. I would visualize him bringing me to the bridge, just above where I would sit and meditate.

The spot I visualize is one that is actually magical for me. There is the nature of the river, the view of the mountain, and I am surrounded by the city I love. I would imagine this very intimate proposal just between us on the bridge. And then all of our friends and family coming out and surrounding us and congratulating us, followed by an awesome engagement celebration dinner. For me, this visualization was about that intimate connection I wanted and being able to have everyone be a part of it.

After a while I got what I needed out of the visualization and I changed my workout routine so I didn't do it anymore. It's important to let the processes go when they are no longer feels juicy or necessary. For me, I got the juice out of the visualization. I had a clear picture in my head so I didn't need to practice it anymore, and I could just let go and send it out to be created.

A year after I had stopped practicing this particular visualization one of my best friends proposed to another one of my best friends, on a bridge over a river, surrounded by their closest friends and family who did not know it was coming! So the intimacy of the moment was there, followed by a celebration dinner with all of us. Evidence! I would like to say my soulmate is sitting next to me right now, but he's not here yet. However based on that big piece of evidence, even though it was two years ago, I know he's close.

If I hadn't noticed this big piece of evidence can you imagine how disappointed I would be right now waiting on him? I know that evidence doesn't lie. It's a sign that what I desire is on its way. I also know that manifestations that involve another human being aren't as cut and dried as some other things, so patience and looking for the evidence is key.

Sometimes evidence is big, like the story above. Sometime it's smaller, like seeing something in a store that is in a picture on your vision board, or having a conversation that mirrors something you have scripted. Learning to see the evidence is important. Writing it down is even more important, because there will be days you will wonder if this is working. On those days, you can flip through your evidence log and remind yourself it is working. Big dreams often require a lot to happen behind the scenes in order to bring them into your reality. Sometimes that takes time. So, seeing *any* evidence keeps you in the right frame of mind.

One way to make sure you are seeing the evidence is to stay connected to your vision. Script a journal entry every day, at minimum for 5-15 minutes, that is from your Champagne Life Days. Script in detail. You might not get past breakfast some days, but you will be in that day. You will be keeping the neural pathways in your brain on track. You will be letting the Universe know that story is still what you desire and that it's coming true. You will be getting more and more familiar with yourself in that story.

Verbally script your Champagne Life Story as much as possible as well. Engage a friend to do interviews, or practice telling them about your Champagne Days as if they are happening today. Again you are putting that information out into the Universe so it can come back to you manifested. The more ways you put it out, the quicker and easier it will manifest into your reality.

You also want to find as many ways as possible to experience your Champagne Days. Continue planning days that mirror your Champagne Days. Take advantage of opportunities to practice and continue looking for ways to experience your Champagne Life.

I took improv classes for a year, and I have a troop I perform with, and I love it. However, that is not why I started doing it. One of the main reasons I started taking improv classes is that taking classes gave me a way to experience being on stage every week. Part of my Champagne Life is being on stage speaking to people. Performing is not the exact same thing as speaking, but being on stage is a way of experiencing what I desire. How can you experience living elements of your Champagne Life in person today? Look for ways to experience your Champagne Days as often as possible.

Another way to experience your Champagne Life as fully as you can is to *be* the person who is going to be living that life as much as possible. Every chance you get, check in and ask, "Would my Champagne Self be doing, thinking or saying this?" If the answer is, "No," change it up. Be, do and act as your Champagne Self. Always act as if you are your Champagne Self, living your Champagne Life.

Acting as if will draw your Champagne Life into reality very quickly. One of the ways I recently acted as my Champagne Self was to sign up to be sent an email every week with the new condos and houses for sale, in the areas in which I want to live, that were at a higher price point. The price point I would be searching in when I was living my Champagne Life (the upleveled version). Each time I would get one of these emails, I would open it as if I was shopping for a bigger place already, and that I had all the money I needed. After about three months of doing this, I found my current dream house. I did not think I was ready, but it was what I wanted and it was being sold for a good price. The money magically worked itself out. This house is one more piece in my Champagne Life puzzle.

Shopping for a new home, I was definitely acting as my Champagne Self. And I had practiced the feeling of having the money so well that when the opportunity arose to get the house, the money itself wasn't an issue. In the beginning I told myself I was going to take $6000 out of savings to practice living my Champagne Life for the next year, because this place is $500 a month more than my budget. Not too long after closing, a way to easily create that $500 a month appeared. When you act as your Champagne Self, living your Champagne Life, things work themselves out – because you have already scripted the story with the most amazing final chapter. (Then you will go on to script a new Champagne Life Story.)

Another way to *act as if* is to tap into your future Champagne Self, the one living your Champagne Life. A workshop participant told me, a few days after she completed the workshop, that she had an interview. She said she just stepped into that future version of herself that she had gotten to know during the workshop, and it worked like a charm. She said she realized, "The person that I want to be is already there, and I can access her anytime." It's hard to access something you are unfamiliar with, but once you know your future Champagne Self, it's easy to tap back into her. It's easy to pull her into your life now, because you know her.

You now have a very clear picture you can tap into, at any moment, that you need to remind yourself what your Champagne Life looks like. You also have that vision to use as a lighthouse. Going forward, only do what you are called to do from that vision. If you "think" you should do something, check in with the vision and see if it's the best next step. *Thinking* you should do something and *knowing* you should are two different things. It is going to be much easier to feel the difference now that you have the story scripted. If you think instead of know, don't do it. That makes your life so much easier, because you don't have to think you should do all these things to "make it happen," – because your story is already happening. It started the minute you started scripting it.

Your story is already scripted. It is already in the process of coming true, which means you can let go of having to *do* more and figure out how to *be* more. The only things you have to do are those things that line up with your story and that you feel called to do. The only thing you have to *be* is your Champagne Self. You do not have to go out looking for more to learn or do. You've got this. Take a deep breath and sit with that for a moment. Your story is already happening.

WHAT COULD GET IN
YOUR WAY?

The biggest obstacle you are going to face in the process of scripting your Champagne Life Story is time. The concentrated three days of creating your script is important for a couple of reasons. The first one is that your brain starts to change in three days. When you finish, your brain will be different. It will know how to think and act out your Champagne Life Story.

The second one is that the longer you spread the experience out over time, the more diluted the story becomes. When you pick up where you left off 20 times, it's a lot different than doing that 5 times. It is the same reason I only write books in 3 days now. They are better, and more cohesive, than when I spread out the writing over four weeks. The concentration of the story is part of what makes it really successful.

The other reason to do it in a concentrated way is that you get to become fully integrated and immersed in "experiencing" it. You are living and breathing your script for three days. The concentration does not allow for fear and doubt to creep in, because you are so focused on what you need to do to script your story.

Committing to a three-day, concentrated time frame makes it less likely for something from your existing life to come up and get in the way. Every day you add to the process is an opportunity for life to happen, interrupting the process, prompting you to put off scripting for one day, and then that becomes two, and then it's very possible that you do not finish the creation phase of your Champagne Life.

Not finishing this project after you start it is actually *worse* than never starting at all. This is because you start with getting really clear about what you desire, and then you script the story to fill in how you are going to get it from where you are now. Not finishing the story and the integration says to your brain and soul, "We can't do this." It is one of those things that you want to go *all in* or not go in at all.

How do you make it work? Pick three days in a row. Put them on your calendar, and make a promise to yourself to finish. You are giving yourself the gift of your time, and the gift of your Champagne Life Story. It is a gift worth giving, and a gift worth the investment. The alternative is to keep trying to get to a destination that you do not have a GPS point for.

Do you want to start driving to Florida, just to turn around and head to Seattle, then change your mind again – and head toward New Mexico? How long will doing it that way take you? It is well worth the investment to create your Champagne Life Story now, so that you are not just driving around aimlessly.

Another thing that could get in your way is thinking that you understand the concept, but being unsure that you can do it on your own. That is normal. It is a big task, and while I believe you can do it on your own, I am also a person who likes to do things like this with someone guiding the process and to keep me on track. I have you covered. I offer virtual and live Script Your Champagne Life workshops. Yes, they require an investment of both time and money. Is it worth the investment if you actually do it and start creating your Champagne Life? What is the cost of wandering to your desired destination? If you can get to your Champagne Life faster and easier, how much is that worth?

The alternative is continuing to try to convince yourself that you can do it on your own. That can be difficult. I understand. You want to do it. You think you can do it and then you get in the middle of it and realize you have questions that you need to be answered before you move ahead. Those thoughts might even keep you from starting. The most important thing is to do it. If you can do it on your own, great. If you want support, get it. It will be one of the best investments you ever make.

Another thing that could get in your way is your fear that once you do it, you won't know how to implement your script. You won't know how to experience your Champagne Life. How will you know if you are being your Champagne Self? You can do this. I know you can. And if you need or want support around this, you can get a year of support with me where we figure out together how to integrate your story into your life so your dream comes true faster.

Something else that is going to happen: You are going to draw in much of your Champagne Story, but you are not going to realize it. The other day, I had a client come to a session feeling like nothing was working. Actually the opposite was happening. Everything was working, she just couldn't see it yet. It became obvious when I pointed it out. Keep an evidence log, so you can go back and see things showing up, and notice all that has appeared out of your Champagne Life.

There's something else that may or may not get in your way. It was a big one for me. When I was creating my Champagne Life, I really wanted to be connected with people and share the journey. You know someone to send a message to about what may look like only a *little* piece of evidence to someone else—but I know is a *big* deal and I wanted to share it with someone who would understand.

Having someone to share the journey makes all the difference. It can feel lonely when things are going really well and you don't have anyone you feel like "gets it" to share with, because you may not know anyone who is consciously creating to the degree that you are practicing. I had, and still have, a couple of really good friends along the way who I can share with. That wasn't always the case though. One year, in January, I set the intention that I would attract friends who supported my business and my dream life.

Cool things happened following that intention. That was the year I met one of my best friends, at a business conference. I connected online with another one of my best friends, and the best coach I know. And that was the year that a friend of mine, who I never thought would become someone I shared my business success with in any way, became that friend and witness for me. She even lived with me for a little bit, and was happy to celebrate every good thing that happened for me and my business.

It took some time for all those things to come together and create the magic support I was looking for. I always wanted a place I could plug in to. I looked for that, and didn't find it. That is why I do group coaching. It provides a place to automatically plug in and be connected. You can create support anyway you desire. I promise. Set the intention and open to inspiration. What you desire will show up. If you would like a place to plug in right now, join the Champagne Life Facebook group by clicking here (https://www.facebook.com/groups/809580085784978/)

You are worthy of living your Champagne Life. Do not let yourself get stuck spinning. Engage a coach for your journey. Spinning your wheels takes time, energy and it costs you money in the long run. I hear it all the time from the women in my year-long coaching program, "This call changed everything. I've been struggling with this and you helped me fix it in five minutes." Spinning in life is like spinning the tires when you are stuck in the mud. You exert a lot of energy that you can't get back, and you don't get anywhere. Eventually, you get out of the car in frustration and miss out on where you wanted to go.

Love yourself enough to get out of the spins quickly. If you are going to invest the time in scripting your Champagne Life Story, invest the money in a coach to support you through the journey. You will get there so much quicker and easier with a coach by your side. Tell your coach that you have read this book and that you are going to script your story or have already done so. Share it with them, and tell them you want support to make it happen. You are going to create a magnificent story. Enroll the support of people worthy of partaking in your story.

The number one thing that has the potential to get in the way of creating and living your Champagne Life Story is what I call the shakiness. When you grow and expand to a new level, you are a lot like a baby learning to walk. When a baby starts to walk (I learned this by watching my niece go through the process) they're not solid on their feet. They wobble. Sometimes they sit down so they don't fall. In the beginning they won't take off unless they know the next place to hold onto is only three steps away, and they are confident they can make it. That's cruising — wanting to spend more time on two feet, but only doing it with tangible support ready at arm's length, or a parent to hold on to their arms and guide them.

Over time, cruisers become more steady. They gain confidence. They feel comfortable walking, and eventually it becomes just as easy and natural as crawling. They become a "walker." This is the same thing that happens when you grow and expand in a really big way. You go from a crawler to a walker and in the middle it is shaky. It doesn't bother a baby to be shaky and unsure when they are getting familiar with walking — they're too busy trying to walk. It does bother adults when they grow and expand and all of a sudden feel shaky and unsure.

You are not unsure. You are doing something that is unfamiliar. It takes time to get to know yourself at the new, expanded level. It takes time to feel confident walking as the new version of yourself. Most people don't realize this happens. When it's happening, it doesn't feel like wobbling. It feels like everything falling apart. It appears like everything is falling apart around you. You might cry a lot and not know why. You might feel emotional, angry or anxious for no reason. You might go from everything being out of this world great — to feeling like every single thing is falling apart, in just a day. It is ok. You are getting familiar with the new you.

It takes time for everything that has come apart and shifted to gel back together in its new form. The shakiness is a good thing, but most people do not recognize it as such. They get scared and feel very alone if they are the only ones in their circle going through this, if everyone else seems to have their feet under them more or less. Not being familiar with what is going on, or that it is common and in fact a good sign, can lead to a downward spiral of "it's not working." Or an undermining of confidence that can also be a hard setback. It is very important that when making such an expansive move, like scripting your Champagne Life Story, you know it's a possibility — and actually a probability — that there will be times when it seems wobbly.

How do you handle the shakiness? Remind yourself that is all it is. When you feel emotional and unsure, be really good to yourself. Let yourself feel the emotions so they can move through you. Take extra good care of yourself during these times, and allow yourself time to integrate with the new you. Be gentle with yourself. Most importantly don't make it mean anything other than you are growing, and that is a good thing.

LEARN MORE ABOUT PUTTING THESE PRINCIPLES INTO ACTION

LISTEN TO Manifest it Now ON ITUNES

WHAT DO YOU HAVE TO LOSE?

You have nothing to lose by committing 3 days to creating a new story. If you are frustrated and or feel stuck, the worst thing that can happen is that you feel the same when you are done. I do not believe that will happen, but if that is the worst thing that can happen to you — it means you really have nothing to lose.

There is no risk in scripting your new story. You get to create it exactly the way you want it. You get to fill in the details. You get to determine the ending. You can keep trying to solve the problems you are experiencing today, or you can create a whole new story, and start living it tomorrow.

Give yourself the greatest gift of all, your Champagne Life Story. It is magical, transformative and much easier then continuing to spin your tires trying to get what you desire through more hard work, trial and error. You deserve a life that you are happy to live, that fills you with joy, that feels effortless and supportive, and lets you have the experiences and the feelings you desire. You are worthy of having it happen quicker and easier than you ever thought possible.

So, are you going to script your Champagne Life Story?

You are beautiful, wonderful and amazing. You have something unique that makes the world a better place. Whether life is good and you want it to be better — or life feels really shitty (pardon my French) at the moment — you deserve the life you have been dreaming of, and *that* life is possible. Whether you started dreaming when you picked up this book, or you have been dreaming for years, that life is closer than it seems right now, and you hold all the power to create it faster and easier than you ever thought possible. I want that for you!

I know what it's like to get up every morning right smack in the middle of my Champagne Life. There is no better feeling than knowing you created a life you truly love living — day in and day out. It's magical. It's wonderful, and it feels so good. I am at a place in my life where I have lived and practiced my dream life so well that there is no way to ever live differently, unless I choose to change the course. My life is a reflection of who I am, and vice versa. This life was waiting for me to come true, and your dream life is waiting for you, too.

I have seen miracles happen. In three days, everything can be different, because if you commit to the process, *you* will be different. When you uncover the future version of yourself, you will be amazed at how your Champagne Life flows to you like champagne flows to the bottom glass of a champagne tower. No force needed. It simply fills the glass.

I have watched more than one person struggle to get the life they desire. I also, personally, remember what it's like to struggle through frustration, and endless work, to get what I wanted, or at least closer. I actually never got there that way, by working harder or struggling more. If you are currently frustrated because you think you are doing everything you can, or you are stuck because you do not know how to move forward, or you are simply ready for *bigger* and *better* — let's do this. Let's script your Champagne Life Story. Let's get you to your *happily ever after* as fast and easy as we can.

You have nothing to lose and everything to gain. If you are unhappy, frustrated, struggling, dancing around the edges, stuck, or ready for more — it is time to script your Champagne Life Story.

Take a moment to visualize the end of your Champagne Life Story. You know — the one where everything works out, you get a life that is even better than you imagined, and the final scene of the movie captures you heading off into the sunset to live that vision. Visualize that final scene in the major motion picture of your life. What does it look like? Who is there? What is happening? What song plays as the scene ends and the credits start? How good would it feel to be living *that* life?

It is time to write the script to that story. If you know you want to script your Champagne Life Story with support from me and other amazing people scripting their Champagne Life Stories, click here (http://www. liveyourchampagnelife.com/script-your-champagne-life-workshop) to join the next workshop.

If you are pretty sure the next best thing for you to do is script your Champagne Life Story, but you have a few questions, schedule a complimentary strategy session by clicking here (http://www.liveyourchampagnelife.com/book-to-discuss-the-script-your-champagne-life-ws) so we can get your questions answered and get you started scripting.

If you are ready to script your Champagne Life Story right now click here (http://www.liveyourchampagnelife.com/lifestyle-design-toolkit) for your complimentary tool kit to support you!

My wish for you is that you get to live a scene out of your Champagne Life Story as soon as possible. I want you to know, with *complete certainty,* that your Champagne Life is around the corner, just like I did when my friends got engaged on a bridge surrounded by their friends.

Come on, let's get you there! Make reservations for your Champagne Life right now by clicking here (http://www.liveyourchampagnelife.com/script-your-champagne-life-workshop).

Cheers to your Champagne Life Story!

IN CASE YOU WERE WONDERING...

As you might have figured out, the love of my life isn't here yet. There is more and more evidence each day that he is on his way. The one thing I have learned in this process is that manifestations that involve another human being are on their own timeframe. Someone else is getting ready for you, too, and you want them to come when *they* are ready as well as you are. When you are waiting for the one, your soulmate, your true love, patience is virtue.

I thought I was doing all the things, in the beginning, to make room for him. I was creating a life "he" would be attracted to, too. What I've learned is that if you create a life you love to live, there is always room for "the one." The more you create a life that reflects who *you* are and how *you* want to live, the easier it will be for him or her to just step into it with you, if they are truly *the one.*

Sometimes waiting sucks. Especially when you do not know when it will be over. When you were a kid, and Christmas (or Hannukah, or Diwali, or Kwanzaa...or your birthday) was coming, you knew how many more days until you got to open your presents. That doesn't happen when you are waiting on the love of your life to show up.

There are ways to make waiting easier, like creating a life you love to live every day, and not waiting to experience your life fully until he or she arrives. That life is your Champagne Single Life, which is coincidentally the working title of my *next* book, where I'll teach you how to clean out the garbage from the past, identify what you want in a partner, and then let go and start living the life of your dreams *right now*.

LISTEN TO
Manifest it Now
ON iTUNES

LEARN MORE
ABOUT
PUTTING
THESE
PRINCIPLES
INTO ACTION

IF YOU ONLY READ ONE CHAPTER, MAKE IT THIS ONE: AUDIO VERSION INSIDE

Thank you so much for purchasing this book. I am so excited that you are going to script your Champagne Life Story. Whether you have completed the book already or not, I'm glad you are reading this chapter!

First, I have created an audio version for you, so that you can *listen* to the book if you prefer. Second, I have created a toolkit to support you in scripting your Champagne Life. Third, I would love to connect with you as you go through the book. The easiest way to do that is by joining the Champagne Life Facebook group. Feel free to share your stories, and post your questions, in the group. I am happy to answer them!

Access to the audio version and the complete toolkit by clicking here: (http://www.liveyourchampagnelife.com/lifestyle-design-toolkit)

Join the Facebook Group by clicking here:

(https://www.facebook.com/groups/809580085784978/) or search for "Champagne Life" on Facebook.

Cheers!

ABOUT THE AUTHOR

Cassie Parks is a Money Maven. She's dedicated to teaching people how to improve their money mindset to increase their financial success. She's also passionate about real estate investing. Utilizing real estate investing, creating a positive money mindset, and leveraging the power of the Law of Attraction, she retired at 32.

Cassie is the creator of the Money, Money, Money Course. It is the only *pay after you manifest* more money course. She is also the author of *Retired at 32* and *Money Mindset for a Champagne Life*.

Teaching people to live their Champagne Life is one of Cassie's passions. She does this through one-on-one coaching, her Champagne and Coffee group coaching, and speaking or doing interviews about her favorite topics. Speaking to audiences about money mindset, real estate investing, creating your own version of success and self-love are some of her favorite topics.

When Cassie isn't teaching the principles of living a Champagne Life, she can be found enjoying the view from her balcony in Downtown Denver, celebrating with friends over champagne, spending time with her family, traveling, performing Improv, or writing in a local coffee shop.

difference press

Difference Press offers entrepreneurs, including life coaches, healers, consultants, and community leaders, a comprehensive solution to get their books written, published, and promoted. A boutique-style alternative to self-publishing, Difference Press boasts a fair and easy-to-understand profit structure, low-priced author copies, and author-friendly contract terms. Its founder, Dr. Angela Lauria, has been bringing to life the literary ventures of hundreds of authors-in-transformation since 1994.

LET'S MAKE A DIFFERENCE WITH YOUR BOOK

You've seen other people make a difference with a book. Now it's your turn. If you are ready to stop watching and start taking massive action, reach out.

"Yes, I'm ready!"

In a market where hundreds of thousands books are published every year and are never heard from again, all participants of The Author Incubator have bestsellers that are actively changing lives and making a difference.

In two years we've created over 134 bestselling books in a row, 90% from first-time authors. We do this by selecting the highest quality and highest potential applicants for our future programs.

Our program doesn't just teach you how to write a book—our team of coaches, developmental editors, copy editors, art directors, and marketing experts incubate you from book idea to published bestseller, ensuring that the book you create can actually make a difference in the world. Then we give you the training you need to use your book to make the difference you want to make in the world, or to create a business out of serving your readers. If you have life-or world-changing ideas or services, a servant's heart, and the willingness to do what it REALLY takes to make a difference in the world with your book, go to http://theauthorincubator.com/apply/ to complete an application for the program today.

*Clarity Alchemy:
When Success Is
Your Only Option*

by Ann Bolender

*Cracking the Code:
A Practical Guide
to Getting You
Hired*

by Molly Mapes

*Divorce to Divine:
Becoming the
Fabulous Person
You Were Intended
to Be*

by Cynthia Claire

*Facial Shift:
Adjusting to an
Altered Appearance*

by Dawn Shaw

*Finding Clarity:
Design a Business
You Love and
Simplify Your
Marketing*

by Amanda H.
Young

*Flourish: Have
It All Without
Losing Yourself*

by Dr. Rachel Talton

*Marketing
To Serve: The
Entrepreneur's
Guide to Marketing
to Your Ideal
Client and Making
Money with Heart
and Authenticity*

by Cassie Parks

*NEXT: How to
Start a Successful
Business That's
Right for You and
Your Family*

by Caroline Greene

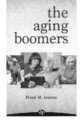

Pain Free: How I Released 43 Years of Chronic Pain

by Dottie DuParcé (Author), John F. Barnes (Foreword)

Secret Bad Girl: A Sexual Trauma Memoir and Resolution Guide

by Rachael Maddox

Skinny: The Teen Girl's Guide to Making Choices, Getting the Thin Body You Want, and Having the Confidence You've Always Dreamed Of

by Melissa Nations

The Aging Boomers: Answers to Critical Questions for You, Your Parents and Loved Ones

by Frank M. Samson

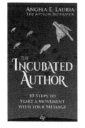

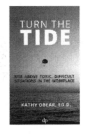

The Incubated Author: 10 Steps to Start a Movement with Your Message

by Angela Lauria

The Intentional Entrepreneur: How to Be a Noisebreaker, Not a Noisemaker

by Jen Dalton (Author), Jeanine Warisse Turner (Foreword)

The Paws Principle: Front Desk Conversion Secrets for the Vet Industry

by Scott Baker

Turn the Tide: Rise Above Toxic, Difficult Situations in the Workplace

by Kathy Obear

Made in the USA
San Bernardino, CA
17 August 2019